CONTENTS

THE CHARACTERS

Judas

For the first time in his life, Judas has a sense of purpose. Will Jesus live up to Judas's expectations?

Jesus

What is Jesus trying to achieve? Will he fulfil Judas's hopes? Does he already know where this friendship will lead?

Simon Peter

Simon Peter is one of Jesus's most trusted disciples. Can such different men as Simon and Judas work well together?

Pharisees

Pharisees are men of God and men of the law. Why might they see Jesus as a threat? Why does Judas want to confront them?

Levi

Levi is a tax collector, hated by the people. What point is Jesus making when he befriends him?

Zacharias

A Jewish priest and a friend of Judas's father, can Zacharias persuade Judas to help him? What does he hope to achieve?

Pontius Pilate

The Roman governor of the province. Will his decision save Judas from the consequences of his own actions?

JUDAS ISCARIOT

Jesus smiled as his mother entertained us with stories about his childhood. 'He was only twelve,' she reminisced, 'but all the men on the temple steps were listening to him. He'd drawn quite a crowd.'

'No,' I gasped involuntarily. Everybody turned to me.

'Are you all right, Judas?' asked Andrew.

'Fine, thanks,' I said, but in truth I was rather shaken. Mary had awakened a long-dormant memory. Twenty years ago, still a boy myself, I had been in that crowd. I had seen Jesus talking to those men on the temple steps.

Like many Jewish boys, I accompanied my father to Jerusalem once a year to take part in the Passover festival, commemorating our people's freedom from slavery in Egypt. That particular year, my father had joined the other priests in the temple, leaving me alone and awkward on the steps.

Another boy was there, about my age. Like me, he was alone. I smiled, unsure what to say. He returned my smile, then turned away to join a group of men. Feeling rather rejected, I watched him. He spoke confidently, and the men listened intently. Why couldn't I be confident like him? The disappointment, longing and jealousy were too painful. I turned my back on him and crept into the temple.

Now, listening to Mary's memories of her son's childhood, I realised that the other boy on the temple steps all those years ago was Jesus himself.

That was when the end of my story was written.

Everyone expected me to follow in my father's footsteps and become a priest, but I was undecided. I felt uncomfortable with some aspects of Jewish law, or at least the way most priests interpreted it. Even in my twenties I was still uncertain. Then one day I met a man who gave me a new sense of purpose. At last I had a direction.

One spring I had accompanied my elderly father on a journey north to visit some relatives. On the way back we planned to rest in Capernaum on the shores of Lake Galilee. Wearily approaching the town, we noticed a crowd gathered on a dusty hillside. As we drew nearer, we could hear a man talking to them.

'Who is that?' I asked one of the listeners.

'Jesus of Nazareth,' he whispered.

Jesus of Nazareth! So this was the man everyone was talking about. I persuaded my father to stay and listen, eagerly pulling him into the crowd.

Jesus's words startled me, made my heart beat faster. Problems which had tormented me for years suddenly seemed simple. No priest had ever made such sense. I felt tears in my eyes. Embarrassed, I wiped them away. I felt I had been searching for this man all my life.

A few months earlier I had visited John the Baptist, a holy man who was calling on people to love God and to keep the laws given to us by Moses. I had thought he might be the one who would deliver our people from the Romans, refresh our laws, and make us a strong and God-fearing nation again.

John himself had made it clear that I was expecting too much of him. 'I am just a voice in the desert,' he told me, 'here to prepare the way for someone greater. When he comes he will baptise you with the Holy Spirit.'

Could Jesus be the man promised by John? Whether he was or not, I wanted to hear more. For the first time in my life I felt certain about something. I needed to follow Jesus.

My father tugged at my sleeve, his frail voice anxious. 'Come away, Judas. This man and his ideas will divide our people. He will only cause trouble.'

I looked at my father. I thought about his insistence on ritual and sacrifice; I thought about the wealth of the synagogues in such a poor land. 'I'm sorry, father,' I whispered, 'but I must go to him. I have no choice.'

Weeping, I turned away from my father and walked towards Jesus. The crowds were already dispersing. Unable to find the right words, I smiled at him.

Jesus seemed to have been expecting me. 'Follow me,' he said.

I did. It might have seemed a simple choice at the time, but – unfortunately for me – nothing is ever simple.

I soon settled into Jesus's group. Some of the men lived in Capernaum, where we stayed in Simon's home and courtyard free of charge. The house, being large enough for small gatherings of people and close to the synagogue, made an ideal base. As Jesus had already made me responsible for our limited supply of money, I was pleased with this economical arrangement.

For months we travelled around Galilee, learning from Jesus as he taught and healed. We relied upon people's generosity for food and shelter. I wasn't used to being without money, and found it very liberating. These were exciting times, full of hope. As Jesus's fame spread it became difficult for us to escape the crowds, but he always refused to send people away. I think he genuinely loved them all.

On one such occasion we were resting indoors. Jesus was deep in discussion with some Pharisees, strict teachers of Jewish law. Outside, as usual, a crowd was gathering. Suddenly, Simon leaped to his feet. 'What's that noise on the roof?'

We looked up to see a paralysed man being lowered from the roof on a stretcher.

His friends had found a way to reach Jesus through the crowds. Jesus seemed impressed by their faith. He touched the man, saying, 'Friend, your sins are forgiven.'

The Pharisees looked uncomfortable. They were men of God, and this seemed wrong to them. 'Surely only God can forgive sins,' they mused.

'You fail to see what true forgiveness looks like,' said Jesus, 'so you refuse to believe. Watch and believe.' Turning to the paralysed man, he said quietly, 'Take up your bed and walk.'

The man, amazed, did as he was bid.

As I said, exciting times.

One of the most exciting things about Jesus was that he was not afraid to challenge people, even figures of authority, about their beliefs and lifestyles. I convinced myself that these were small steps towards great change.

One afternoon we passed the booth of a tax collector called Levi. Tax collectors were hated by the Jewish people because they gave our money to the Romans, and mixed with non-Jews, which was forbidden by law.

Jesus called out to Levi those now familiar words, 'Follow me.' To the surprise of everyone around us, Levi immediately got up and ran to Jesus's side, leaving his money on the table. That evening Levi invited Jesus to join him and his friends, most of whom were also tax collectors, in a celebratory meal.

Some of the Pharisees heard about Levi, and challenged Jesus. 'Why do you eat and drink with sinners?' they asked, unsmiling.

Jesus explained, 'It is the sick who need a doctor, not the healthy. I am here to help sinners – the righteous do not need such help.' This was radical!

Jesus's actions plunged us into another area of controversy. Rabbis and Pharisees had for years been debating which of two contradictory demands should take precedence. Our laws tell us to rest on the Sabbath, but we also need to survive and to respond to people's needs.

I remember one Sabbath we were walking through a farmer's field. As we walked, we plucked a few ears of wheat, rubbed them to get rid of the chaff, and chewed the grain inside.

16

'Oh no, here's trouble,' muttered James, pointing to the edge of the field, where two Pharisees had stopped in their tracks to watch us. One of the Pharisees called out, 'Why are you harvesting on the Sabbath?'

I laughed, and muttered 'Don't be so ridiculous', but Jesus touched my arm to silence me. He approached the Pharisees.

He explained to them that looking after others, like feeding people when they are hungry, must sometimes take precedence over strict religious law. He reminded them that even famous King David had technically broken the law when he once fed his hungry men with the bread reserved for the Sabbath. He looked them in the eye. 'And I,' he said quietly, 'am lord of the Sabbath.'

This was very daring, some might say arrogant. This was exciting. Jesus was publicly claiming authority over the law.

Jesus also attracted criticism for healing

on the Sabbath, but it never stopped him. 'Is it really wrong to do good and to save life on the Sabbath?' he challenged those who questioned him.

He always knew what to say – unlike me.

One calm evening we were in the hills praying. Jesus drew twelve of us close to him. 'There is too much work for me to do alone,' he confided. 'Soon I must rely on you to tell people about me and heal the sick.'

I looked at the other eleven men. What a strange collection! We were from such varied backgrounds;

we had different strengths, different ideas. Some of us were more driven, some – dare I say it – more intelligent than others. I looked at Simon, Andrew, James and John. They were only fishermen. Could Jesus *really* rely on *all* of us?

As Jesus led us down to the crowd below, he put his arm around my shoulders. I swelled with pride that he was singling me out from the others. Perhaps he shared my doubts about their abilities. Perhaps this was his way of expressing special favour. In hindsight, however, I think he had read my mind and felt sorry for me.

Jesus began to preach. His words, though addressed to the crowd, held special significance for the twelve of us he had just chosen. 'Blessed are you who are poor,' he assured, 'for yours is the kingdom of God. Blessed are you who hunger, for you will be fed.' He taught that those who grieved would be comforted, and that the pure, the good and the peacemakers would all be welcomed by God. Looking meaningfully towards us, he affirmed 'Blessed are you when men hate you because of me.' A chill ran through me.

Though Jesus's message was straightforward, his demands were often difficult.

'Love your enemies,' he preached. 'If you only care for those who care for you, what credit is that to you? Even sinners can do that much! You must learn to treat everybody as you would like them to treat you. Forgive other people, and you will be forgiven.' He paused to take a sip of water, then looked meaningfully round the crowd. 'And be very careful not to judge others; if you do, you risk being judged in the same way.'

Was he looking at me when he said that? I shrank back a little, but he caught my eye. 'How is it that you people can comment so readily on the speck of dust in your brother's eye, yet manage to overlook the plank lodged in your own?'

Jesus followed this with a parable. Parables, apparently simple stories with a message that often seemed puzzling or shocking, were his way of helping ordinary people – including fishermen like Simon – to understand.

'The person who understands my words and puts them into practice is like a man who builds

a house with deep foundations on solid rock. When the flood comes, the torrent strikes their house, but because it is so well built the water hardly shakes it. The person who understands my words yet fails to live by them' – surely he wasn't looking at me again – 'is like a man who builds a house on the sand, with no foundations. As soon as the torrent strikes, the house collapses.'

Did Jesus mean that, the moment trouble comes, such an insecure man might also collapse?

Returning to the seashore at Capernaum, we were approached by some Jewish elders. 'A centurion's servant is sick, can you come and heal him?' Worried that Jesus might hesitate to help a Roman, they added, 'This centurion has been very good to our people,' but Jesus was already on his way. As we neared the centurion's house we met a messenger. Jesus read aloud what the centurion had written – 'I do not deserve to have you in my home. You do not need to come. Just say the word and my servant will be healed.'

Jesus turned to us. 'Let me tell you,' he said seriously, 'I have not found faith like this among my own people, let alone the Romans.'

A Roman with greater faith than a Jew? I wasn't sure how I felt about that. The next day, however, when we heard that the servant was well again, I was forced to reconsider.

All in all I was reconsidering a great deal. Most Pharisees, like my father, were good men, but they tended towards an inflexible adherence to Jewish law. I often felt sad when I thought of my father. I had left him because Jesus offered a more compassionate alternative. I remembered my early expectations that Jesus would challenge the authorities. I was beginning to grow less certain.

From Capernaum we travelled to Nain, where a Pharisee invited us to dine with him. As we ate, a woman entered the room and knelt beside Jesus. I recognised her face from the morning's crowd, where I had noticed her neighbours shunning her, whispering the word 'sinner'. Now, the weeping woman soaked Jesus's feet with tears which she wiped away with her hair. She then rubbed perfumed ointment onto his feet, and I heard her say quietly, 'Lord, please forgive my sins.'

It was rather embarrassing. I wondered how much she had paid for the ointment. She could have given the money to the poor instead. We watched in silence until the Pharisee said to Jesus, 'If you really were the messiah, you would know that this woman is a sinner.'

Jesus turned to him. I sighed – another parable. 'Two men owed money to a money lender. One owed five hundred coins, the other just fifty. Neither could afford to repay him, so he cancelled both their debts. Which of them was more grateful?'

'The one who had owed more, of course.'

'That's right,' replied Jesus. 'You didn't even offer me water to wash my feet when I arrived, but this woman washed my feet with her tears and dried them with her hair; she kissed my feet and anointed them with perfume. She had the least, but gave the most. She knows how to love, and her many sins have been forgiven.' He smiled at the woman. 'Your faith has saved you,' he said gently. 'Go in peace.'

I enjoyed the look of shock, or was it anger too, that I saw in the Pharisee's face.

We were gradually making our way south towards Jerusalem, teaching and healing in the towns on our way. Somewhere on our travels, Jesus had driven many demons out of a woman called Mary Magdalene. Since then, Mary and some of her friends had been financially supporting our work, and Mary often joined us. As I was still responsible for our money, I appreciated their help, although it felt strange to rely on women.

As I have already said, Jesus often taught in parables to help people think for themselves, and not just follow the laws blindly. I remember one parable about a man sowing grain. Some of the grain fell on rocky ground, where it could not take root, while some fell amongst weeds, which choked the young seedlings. Some grain, however, fell in good soil and grew well.

'I don't understand,' I remember Simon saying. 'What can I learn from that?'

'The grain sown on rocky ground is like people who hear the word of God but ignore it,' Jesus explained. 'The grain choked by weeds is like the people who hear what God says and try to live by it, but fail when the going gets too hard.' Why did he look at me; was it because he thought I might fail if I was tested? 'And, of course,' he smiled at Simon, 'the grain that grows well is like the people who hear what God has to say and have the strength and understanding to live up to it.'

On another occasion, a lawyer asked Jesus a question. 'You talk a lot about loving my neighbour,' he said, 'but who exactly is my neighbour? Just the people who live nearby?'

'A man was travelling from Jerusalem to Jericho,' began Jesus, 'when he was attacked by robbers who beat him, took everything he had, and left him naked and dying on the roadside. The first person to pass by was a Levite.' Levites were often temple assistants, people we respected. 'The Levite saw the wounded man, but he walked on without helping him. After a long time, just when the traveller was giving up hope, a Samaritan came along.' We all knew that most Jews dislike the people of Samaria, who have strange ways of worshipping and dress differently from us. 'Well,' Jesus continued, 'when the Samaritan saw the desperate traveller he stopped, bandaged his wounds, lent him his cloak, and took him to an inn, where he paid for him to be looked after.'

'So here is my question,' Jesus looked directly at the lawyer. 'Which do you think was the traveller's true neighbour? The supposedly friendly Levite, or the supposedly untrustworthy Samaritan?'

'I understand now,' said the lawyer humbly. 'Everyone is my neighbour.'

One day Jesus gathered the twelve of us together. 'You are now ready. Go and preach my message, and heal the sick. You have God's authority.'

As Jesus warned us about the dangers that we might face, I looked around the group. Some looked excited, others looked scared. Simon was listening intently like a faithful dog. It was difficult to imagine Simon teaching anyone anything. Though he was eager to please, he often struggled to understand what Jesus was saying.

That evening two sisters, Mary and Martha, invited us to dinner. Martha bustled around preparing food and making the house comfortable, but Mary knelt at Jesus's feet, listening carefully to his words. I noticed Martha looking increasingly exasperated. Eventually, her face red and her voice tight, she strode into the room. 'It isn't fair,' she said. 'My sister has left me to do all the work. Tell her she must help me.'

'Martha,' said Jesus, 'I understand that you have a lot to worry about, but Mary has identified the one thing that is really important. It will not be taken from her.'

This seemed rather unfair. Most of the things Martha was doing did need to be done, though I thought she could have left some of her jobs to listen to Jesus. I sympathised with Martha, because I was always the one who had to find money and food for our group to live on. Some of us are burdened with practicalities, even if we might prefer to concentrate on spiritual things.

That night, Jesus taught Mary and Martha the simple prayer he taught all his followers. 'Our father in heaven, holy is your name. Your kingdom will come and your will must be done. Give us each day our daily bread. Forgive us our sins as we forgive those who sin against us. Lead us not into temptation, and deliver us from evil. The kingdom, the power, and the glory are all yours, now and for ever.'

Prayer was more important than food to Jesus. He insisted that God would always respond to prayer. Just as a good parent provides a child with what is needed, he explained, so God will always provide for us. He taught us to base all our prayers on this one simple one, and to talk to God as a child would talk to a parent. What a contrast with the elaborate prayers the Pharisees taught!

Everything Jesus taught made sense, but I was troubled. What was his ultimate goal? He told us that when we reached Jerusalem he would suffer and die. What would be the point in that? We hadn't achieved anything significant yet, and time was running out.

More and more often, Jesus accused some of the Pharisees of wickedness. 'Woe to you experts in the law,' he warned. 'You ignore justice and hide the keys to heaven.' I agreed with him – after all, this was partly why I had left my father. Yet angering the Pharisees with accusations and insults seemed petty and counterproductive. Surely we should either work with the Pharisees to improve things, or confront them directly. The middle way we seemed to be adopting was simply frustrating.

As we continued towards Jerusalem, I felt an increasing sense of urgency. It was becoming more and more difficult to accept the passivity of Jesus's teaching.

I think we were in Pella when a man asked Jesus to help him sort out his inheritance issues with his brother. As so often, Jesus responded with a parable.

'A man worked hard and stored up wealth so that he could live more easily in the future. But it was all in vain, because he died while he was still gathering together enough money.' He turned to the small crowd that had gathered. 'Beware of all kinds of greed. You mustn't worry about what you will eat or what you will wear. Look at the birds. They do not sow or reap, yet God still feeds them, and you are much more valuable than birds. The lilies in the field do not make clothes, yet they are always dressed in splendour. If that is how God clothes the flowers, how much more will he clothe you? You have far too little faith! Give your possessions to the poor – your heavenly father will give you all that you need.'

This was reassuring, even inspiring, pointing us towards spiritual rather than tangible wealth. Nevertheless, if we were going to eat tonight I needed to go and find us some food. The words, clever though they were, were just words. What about some action?

Jesus had high expectations. He said that people should give up everything they had, including their family, to follow him. That's what I had done the day I turned my back on my father. Jesus also said that we should be prepared to die for him. A little more difficult, I thought. What can dying achieve?

But all in all, I enjoyed the simple lifestyle. I didn't need my father's wealth, and I never doubted the wisdom of Jesus's teaching. I grew to believe that Jesus was right to make God's forgiveness and love available to everyone.

'Suppose you had a hundred sheep, and lost one of them,' he taught one day. 'Would you not

leave the ninety-nine and keep looking for the lost sheep until you found it?'

People nodded.

'And when you found it, wouldn't you carry it home, overjoyed that the lost sheep was safe and well?'

More nods.

Jesus explained. 'There is more joy in heaven over one sinner who repents than ninety-nine good people who do not need to repent.'

He then told a story about a son who asked his father for his share of his inheritance, which he then wasted. This prodigal son, reduced to nothing, returned to his father, expecting to be punished. But his father was thrilled to see him, and organised a celebratory feast to welcome him home.

To Jesus, every sinner was a lost sheep, a prodigal son. He would bring them home.

Although we almost always travelled as a group, I sometimes felt lonely. There was no one with whom I could share my doubts and confusion about what we were trying to achieve. I had accepted that we weren't going to challenge Roman rule, but I was increasingly concerned that we didn't even seem to be moving towards direct confrontation with the Jewish authorities.

One day, Jesus asked us all who we thought he was. Simon immediately answered, 'You are the son of the living God.' Jesus was pleased, and from then on called Simon 'Peter', after the Greek word for 'rock'. 'Those who recognise who I am will be the rock on which I will build my church,' said Jesus. From then on, Simon Peter's confidence grew while mine seemed to diminish.

I remembered John the Baptist's promise, that a greater man was coming.

Was Jesus this man? I had never been sure, and still could not share the certainty enjoyed by the others. One day, somebody asked Jesus precisely when the kingdom of God would come on earth. At last, I thought, something specific.

'The kingdom of God is already within you', said Jesus. I sort of understood, but it was never quite enough. It was too internal. Jesus continued, 'The son of God will come like lightning flashing in the sky, but first he must suffer at the hands of his own generation.'

What did that mean? That his goals would only be achieved by his own death?

So much had happened since I first met Jesus, but nothing could have prepared me for the next few days. We finally reached the outskirts of Jerusalem. James and John found a colt for Jesus to ride into the city. We walked behind, singing psalms of expectation. But my heart was not in my song. My expectations were low.

Excited, optimistic crowds lined our route to the temple, joining our psalms and spreading palm branches in our path. The rest of the group were clearly exhilarated by our triumphal arrival in Jerusalem, and my mood improved. The psalms voiced Jewish hopes, and the palm is our national symbol. Perhaps the authorities would consider this a challenge. They must now feel threatened. Surely they would have to act.

When we reached the temple, Jesus looked in horror at what was going on there. It looked more like a market place than a temple. At dinner that evening, Jesus outlined a plan. 'We need to reclaim the temple as a place of prayer,' he said. My heartbeat quickened – he was going to mount a challenge!

All Jews had to pay temple tax and buy animals for sacrifice. For both we needed special silver coins. The only place to exchange our money for these coins was the temple, and the exchange rate was weighted heavily in favour of the money-changers. The poor were being robbed – in the temples.

As Jesus explained his plan, my father's words echoed in my head – 'He will cause division.' I felt a thrill of anticipation, swiftly and confusingly followed by a heavy sense of dread.

When we arrived at the temple the next morning, we found an elderly woman trying to exchange her money. She wept as the money-changer refused to give her a fair rate. Jesus approached the table. I held my breath, awed by his controlled anger. Using very little force, Jesus simply lifted the side of the table, sending the silver coins clattering across the floor. The money-changer stared, open-mouthed.

We knew what we had to do. We crashed other tables onto their sides; coins cascaded to the ground. We overturned the benches of men selling doves for sacrifice. Action at last! We caused chaos! Animals ran wild. Money-dealers scrabbled around on the ground, trying to catch their clattering coins. Angry men tried to stop us; others cheered us on. Violence seemed inevitable.

In the midst of the chaos, Jesus strode to the top of the steps. His authoritative voice silenced the din. 'Is it not written in the scriptures that the temple should be a house of prayer for all the nations? You have turned it into a den of thieves!' Noticing a large group of priests moving threateningly towards him, Jesus warned his listeners, 'Do not allow yourselves to be turned away from God.'

In the tense silence that followed, I was surprised to recognise a priest standing next to me. It was Zacharias, one of my father's friends. 'Well, Judas,' he smirked, 'that was rather dramatic. You must be pleased.'

I nodded, my jaw tense.

'Of course, it will make no difference.'

'Maybe not immediately,' I muttered through gritted teeth, 'but soon we shall free our people from oppression.'

'You fool,' sneered Zacharias. 'Jesus and his naive ideas will never challenge any authority.

Have you followed
him for three
years without
understanding
his words? Haven't
you heard him say,
"My kingdom is
not of this world,"
and "give to Caesar what
belongs to Caesar"?'

I was stunned. Zacharias was right. All
along Jesus had been telling us that real change
comes from within us, not from outside. But I
hadn't wanted to hear.

'Jesus will never make any real difference,'
continued Zacharias. 'In fifty years, no one will
even remember his name. Or yours.'

I unclenched my fists and walked away.
I needed to think.

Jesus preached in the temple for several days. Afraid to confront such a popular man, the priests tried to catch him out with trick questions. Jesus always silenced them with his answers. This intellectual sparring was clever, but it left me feeling empty. Words, words, words.

When I had believed that Jesus would match his words with action, I had applauded everything he said, but now I was worried. Hundreds of people were leaving their families to follow Jesus, just as I had done, and giving away all that they owned. People were suffering in order to follow him. For what purpose? What suffering lay ahead for those who continued to follow him? I began to feel that Jesus needed to be stopped, both for his own sake and for the safety of his followers.

Zacharias sought me out. 'Your friend is dangerous,' he frowned. 'He must be stopped.' This reflected my own thoughts so closely that I was shocked. Zacharias's frown melted into a smile. 'Come and talk to my friends.'

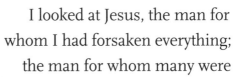

I looked at Jesus, the man for
whom I had forsaken everything;
the man for whom many were
prepared to die; the
man who was unlikely
to achieve anything
unless forced into direct
confrontation; the man
who had chosen Simon as his 'rock'.
The familar feelings of disappointment, longing
and jealousy were too painful.

I turned my back on him and followed
Zacharias into the temple.

The time to celebrate the Passover arrived, but I
didn't feel celebratory. Days before, in return for
thirty pieces of silver, I had promised the priests
that I would find them an opportunity to arrest
Jesus. That should force him into action. If not,
at least his dangerous inaction would be stopped.

45

Jesus sent Simon Peter and John to find and prepare a room for our meal that night. As usual it was my job to provide the food. It was a cosy room that they found, just big enough for the thirteen of us, with a low table and couches on three sides. Jesus invited me to share his couch, a place of honour. I felt very uncomfortable, knowing what I had to do.

Before we ate, Jesus said, 'I am pleased to eat this Passover meal with you all before I have to suffer.' I shivered. Jesus's references to his future suffering took on a new meaning now I had made my deal with the temple priests.

Jesus picked up some bread and gave thanks for it. Giving us each a piece, he said, 'This is my body, given for you. Do this to remember me.' He then picked up the cup of wine. 'This is God's new promise to you, in my blood.'

I dipped my bread into the wine with Jesus, then rested

my hand upon the table alongside his and John's. Quiet moments passed before Jesus said softly, 'The hand of the man who will betray me is with mine on the table.' I quickly moved my hand away. 'Woe to that man who betrays me,' he said quietly.

John was horrified. 'Is it me?' he asked.

I felt dizzy. I could not look at Jesus. 'Surely not me, Rabbi?'

Jesus whispered into my ear, 'I shall go to the Mount of Olives afterwards to pray.'

He knew! He knew what I was going to do! After the meal I stumbled down the stairs. Tears blurred my vision and emotion blurred my thoughts. I ran to where the chief priest lived. I kept my promise.

'We need you with us, to identify him,' insisted a guard.

'No, please, no!'

It was a miserable walk to the Mount of Olives. The moon was bright, and the guards were noisy in their armour. Jesus must have seen and heard us. I'm sure he could have escaped if he had wanted to. I wish that he had.

When we arrived he was standing calmly, waiting. Then I saw the others. Simon Peter was rubbing his eyes as if he had been asleep.

A guard pushed me roughly forward. 'Rabbi!' I greeted Jesus, identifying him in just one word. Then I kissed his cheek.

'Judas,' he smiled, 'do you hand me over with a kiss?'

The dreamlike, dreadful stillness was suddenly broken. The disciples and the guards prepared to fight, but Jesus raised his hand to calm them. He asked the priests sadly, 'Is it because I am leading a rebellion that you have come with swords? I was with you in the temple courts every day, yet you did not lay a hand on me. Now darkness reigns, and this is your hour.' Then he allowed himself to be led away. His friends fled. I wanted to run, but the guards held me.

The hours that followed were the worst of my life. I hadn't given much thought to what might happen to Jesus. I suppose I had hoped that my actions would make Jesus do something decisive, something that would really change things. Instead, I had to watch while he endured the most sickening brutality. The guards insulted him and beat him. They blindfolded him, hit him and taunted him.

Why didn't he save himself? I struggled to convince myself that there were good reasons for what I had done.

It was daybreak when they tried Jesus. 'Are you really the son of God?' they asked.

'You say that I am,' answered Jesus.

That was enough. 'Blasphemy!' cried the chief priest triumphantly. 'We have heard it from his own lips! What more do we need? Take him to Pilate!'

Pontius Pilate was the Roman prefect of the province. I followed as they led Jesus to Pilate's palace. 'This man opposes the payment of taxes to Caesar and claims to be a messiah, a king,' the priests told Pilate. I gasped at their lies. The irony struck me with terrible force. I had betrayed this selfless, compassionate man because he had failed to do either of the things of which he was now accused.

Pilate looked carefully at Jesus. 'Are you the King of the Jews?'

'So you say.'

Pilate turned to the priests and the crowd that had followed. 'I find no basis for a charge against him.'

This caused uproar, the priests insisting that Jesus had tried to stir up rebellion. Pilate, growing uncomfortable, continued to argue that there was no charge to be answered. Eventually, seeking to pass the burden of responsibility to somebody else, Pilate sent Jesus to King Herod, who was in Jerusalem for the Passover. Herod sent Jesus straight back to Pilate. Wearily, Pilate addressed the crowd outside his palace. 'I find no basis for charges against this man. Neither does Herod. To appease you, I will punish him then release him, but I will not kill him.'

The crowd roared its dissatisfaction. Why was I being forced to endure this? I tried not to catch Jesus's eye. I had kept my promise. Seeing Jesus humiliated was dreadful; seeing the way he looked at me was far, far worse. I wanted to return my money to the priests, to undo what I had done. It was too late.

Alongside Jesus stood another prisoner, Barabbas, a rebel accused of murder. Pilate turned to the crowd. 'I will release one of these men. You must choose who will be freed.' I shared Pilate's undisguised hope that they would release Jesus; that this terrible course of events would end, but the crowd's chant of 'Release Barabbas, release Barabbas' was as deafening as it was shocking. The mounting hysteria became more bloodthirsty, the chant changing to 'Crucify Jesus!' My whole body shook. Crucifixion!

Pilate tried to quieten them. 'Why?' he asked.

He was answered with a crescendo of chanting – 'Crucify him!' Pilate had no choice. Symbolically, he asked for a basin of water to wash his hands of the whole business.

Had I had a choice? Could I now, like Pilate, wash the guilt from my hands?

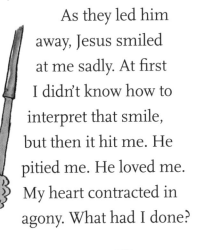

As they led him away, Jesus smiled at me sadly. At first I didn't know how to interpret that smile, but then it hit me. He pitied me. He loved me. My heart contracted in agony. What had I done?

They killed him this afternoon. The sky grew as dark as my soul.

How can I live with such guilt? Can I find comfort in the possibility that this was God's plan, that I had no choice? Maybe our goals will be better served by Jesus's death than by his life, as he so often hinted. Is this how he will bring his lost sheep home? I don't fully understand.

Or perhaps Zacharias's words will turn out to be true – 'He will never make any real difference. In fifty years no one will even remember his name. Or yours.'

I will not be there to find out.

TAKING THINGS FURTHER

The real read

This *Real Reads* volume of *Judas Iscariot* is our interpretation of the events of the New Testament, told from the perspective of one of the most significant participants. In writing this account of Judas's life, we have used evidence from the gospel according to Luke. This is one of the four gospels – the first four books of the New Testament.

It is important to acknowledge that all four gospels were written after Jesus's death, and that the writers had different aims in mind – although they all wanted to engender faith in the reader that Jesus was the Son of God. The first three gospels – Matthew, Mark and Luke – are called 'the synoptic gospels'. They were probably written between forty and sixty years after the crucifixion. The gospel according to John, written later, is significantly different.

Sometimes, the four gospels' accounts of events differ considerably. At first this made our task rather difficult, until we realised that what we needed to do was present the New Testament as it is, rather than to weave a path of our choice between the gospels. Therefore, if you read all six books in the *Real Reads* New Testament series, you may well notice some of the apparent contradictions and inconsistencies that are present in the Bible itself.

There is a gospel of Judas, discovered in Egypt in the 1970s. Although a great deal of controversy surrounds this text, it has been radiocarbon dated to around the late third century. We considered drawing upon evidence from the gospel of Judas for this *Real Reads* version, but decided that our job was to stay faithful to the recognised New Testament.

As with all the other characters in this series, we do not really know what Judas thought of the events through which he lived. Using thorough research and paying close attention to the Bible account, we have tried to imagine what he might have been like, and what he might have thought.

This *Real Reads Judas Iscariot* does not cover all the events of the New Testament. Reading the other five books in the series will bring you closer to an understanding of the complete story. You may then want to read the New Testament itself. We recommend that you read either the *New International Version* or *The Youth Bible*, details of which are given below.

Biblical sources

Although *Judas Iscariot* is based on the story as told in the gospel of Luke, there are a few places where we have drawn on other sources.

On the *Real Reads* website you will find an online concordance (www.realreads.co.uk/ newtestament/concordance/judas). A 'bible concordance' is an indexing tool which allows you to see how the same words, sentences and passages appear in different versions and translations of the Bible. This online concordance will direct you from events in the *Real Reads* version back to their biblical sources, so you can see clearly where each part of our story is drawn from.

Life in
New Testament times

The main events of Judas's life took place in
Palestine, a long narrow area of land bordered
to the west by the Mediterranean Sea and to the
east by the Transjordanian Desert. Some parts
of Palestine were desert, some were hill country,
some rich pasture land, and some uncultivated
wilderness.

The Jews considered Palestine to be their
'promised land', promised to them by God. Moses
had led them there from slavery in Egypt. The
area was mainly Jewish, with synagogues and
temples. Nevertheless, it is interesting that most
of Jesus's ministry took place around the Sea of
Galilee, an area with a mixed population of Jews
and Gentiles, and a reputation for political unrest.

Although Palestine was Jewish land, it was
part of the Roman Empire and under Roman
control. The Jews resented paying taxes to
Rome. During Jesus's lifetime, there was
considerable conflict between the Jews and their

N

W   E

S

Capernaum •

SEA
OF
GALILEE

GALILEE

Nazareth •

Nain •

Pella •

SAMARIA

RIVER JORDAN

PALESTINE

Jericho •

Jerusalem •

•

Bethany

10   20 miles

DEAD
SEA

Roman rulers. Some Jews must have hoped that Jesus would help to overthrow the Romans. This helps to explain why the Romans might have been nervous of the crowds following Jesus.

The Romans used the existing Jewish authorities to help to govern their subjects. This gave further power and influence to the Jewish leaders. As with any group given such powers, some of these leaders used their influence for the good of the people, some used it corruptly.

Jews of the time, as is still the case for many orthodox Jews today, followed very strict laws, which Judas would have studied as a boy. The Old Testament tells the story of how these laws, the Torah, were handed down from God to Moses. Pharisees were teachers of the law who felt responsible for ensuring that people kept the laws. The Pharisees were very concerned when Jesus seemed to challenge the Torah, though many ordinary Jews would have welcomed the promise of a less authoritative regime.

Finding out more

We recommend the following books and websites to gain a greater understanding of the New Testament.

Books

We strongly recommend that you read the rest of the *Real Reads* New Testament series, as the six narratives interlock to give a more complete picture of events. These are *Jesus of Nazareth*, *Mary of Galilee*, *Simon Peter*, *Mary Magdalene* and *Paul of Tarsus*.

- *New Century Youth Bible*, Authentic Lifestyle, 2007.

- Sally Lloyd-Jones, *The Jesus Storybook Bible: Every Story Whispers his Name*, Zondervan, 2007.

- *People in the Life of Jesus*, Colin Lumsden, Day One Publications, 2003.

- Stephen Adly Guirgis, *The Last Days of Judas Iscariot*, Methuen, 2008.

Websites

- www.bbc.co.uk/religion/religions/christianity/history/whokilledjesus_1.shtml
This interesting and accessible assessment of the parties involved suggests that Judas's involvement was less important than is often accepted.

- www.gospel-mysteries.net/judas-iscariot.html
Some interesting possibilities about Judas.

- www.localhistories.org/new
Brief but useful descriptions of many aspects of everyday life in New Testament times.

TV and film

- *Jesus Christ Superstar*, directed by Norman Jewison. Universal Pictures UK, 2005. This screen version of the 1970s rock opera by Tim Rice and Andrew Lloyd Webber focuses on the relationship between Jesus and Judas.

- *Jesus of Nazareth*, directed by Franco Zeffirelli. ITV DVD, 1977. A six and a half hour mini-series.

Food for thought

Here are some things to think about if you are reading *Judas Iscariot* alone, ideas for discussion if you are reading it with friends.

Starting points

● How would you describe Judas before he decides to follow Jesus? Why can't he decide what to do with his life?

● The words 'longing', 'disappointment' and 'jealousy' appear on pages 8 and 45. Why do you think Judas is experiencing these feelings so strongly on each occasion?

● Can you find examples of Judas's admiration and love for Jesus?

● Can you find examples of Judas's hopes and expectations concerning Jesus?

● What does Judas think about Simon Peter?

- List some of the lessons Jesus teaches people. Can you think of examples of what these lessons might mean in everyday life?

- What evidence is there that Judas became disappointed with Jesus?

- How did you feel about Judas at the end of the book?

Group activities

- With a group of friends, act out the Passover meal in Jerusalem. Give each other advice on how the characters were feeling.

- Imagine Judas's conversation with Zacharias when he follows him into the temple. Can you write it as a short drama and act it out?

- Starting on page 45, take turns reading to the end of the book. Whoever is reading is Judas. Stop at different points in the story and interview Judas about his feelings at that point.